# INSPIRATIONAL FOOTBALL STORIES FOR YOUNG READERS

## 12 UNBELIEVABLE TRUE TALES TO INSPIRE AND AMAZE YOUNG FOOTBALL LOVERS

**Mike Johnson**

ISBN: 979-8-89095-002-4

# CONTENTS

# ATTENTION:

**DO YOU WANT MY FUTURE BOOKS AT
HEAVY DISCOUNTS AND EVEN FOR FREE?**

HEAD OVER TO WWW.SECRETREADS.COM
AND JOIN MY SECRET BOOK CLUB!

# INTRODUCTION

The sport of professional football is one of brutality, strength, athleticism, skill, and finesse. Groups of men battle in the dirt, wind, rain, and snow for the opportunity to win a 'Super Bowl' title. And if they do not win, they come back again and again until their bodies cannot keep up. On its face, football is a tenacious and inspiring game. The self-discipline and mental strength required to execute a game plan are immense.

Quarterbacks have to make quick decisions at the line of scrimmage while their linemen figure out how best to protect them. Tight ends and wide receivers need to be faster and more agile than their defenders, all in the hope that the ball might come their way. Running backs look for holes in the defense where they might run and escape tacklers. Defenders do their best to stop their opponents in every facet of the game, striving to steal the ball back in the process. The game is a battle in every sense of the word, and the players are warriors on the battlefield.

Today's game focuses more on the speed and skill near the sidelines, while games of years past often relied on winning at the line of scrimmage. How a team goes about winning a game, there is a great inspiration to be found at every position, every story of the game. In these pages, we'll examine some of the most inspirational moments and individuals, including some who never had the privilege of playing a single snap of professional football. We'll look at players, coaches, personalities, and owners around the game and how they all made impacts on those around them.

Whether they made inspirational choices on the field, in the front office, or in their homes, good people have made positive changes in the game, and thus in this country's culture. We'll see how a group of owners brought about the induction of the 'Super Bowl', how a kicker broke records without any toes, and even how dynasties can be born within a single family.

This book has those stories and more, packed full of information and tidbits that are sure to entertain and inspire.

# CHAPTER 1:

# TOM DEMPSEY

When it comes to the game of football, one of the most unheralded but highest-scoring positions is that of the kicker. And when it comes to kickers, you don't have to look very far to find one of the most inspiring stories in football history. Tom Dempsey was an NFL kicker for 11 seasons, with his rookie campaign in 1969, and his story is one that many look to for inspiration.

There's quite a lot of inspiration in Tom's life story, but before we get to his NFL career, let's start at the beginning.

Tom was born in Milwaukee, Wisconsin, in 1947. That by itself is not inspiring, but the circumstances of his birth contain the first elements of an inspirational career and life. When Tom was born, his body did not develop fingers on his right hand, nor any toes on his right foot. As a young boy, Tom struggled with the idea that he would not be able to do the same things as other kids.

One day when Tom was struggling to build something, he was ready to give up on the project. Dejected, he told his father how he felt, and his father gave him some sound advice: "Boy, you never say can't. You may have to do something differently, but you can do it."

That idea stuck in Tom's mind, and it helped him find a way forward. Wearing a shoe specially designed for his foot, he began playing football in high school. He was a big kid, too, so he played defense and served as the team's kicker. With some success at the high school level, he moved on to play at Palomar College.

After finishing college, he went undrafted in 1968 but he did earn a tryout with the Green Bay Packers, his home team.

However, when Tom attended that tryout, he did not find instant success. When it came time to run drills and test his skill as a defensive player, up against several others who wanted to make the team and live their dreams, Tom found out the hard way that the NFL was a different world. He was basically flattened by the bigger, stronger players at every turn.

Some players never make it to a college team. Even more who never make the jump to the professional level. It should not have been a surprise that Tom was just another player that didn't have what it takes to make that transition. Very few have it. However, Tom had something that many others do not: he had the will to succeed.

From that moment on, Tom decided that it would perhaps be best if he moved on from playing defense. Instead, he decided to focus on kicking. He didn't give up on his football dream, no. Instead, he looked to the other football skill that he had developed, even if it wasn't the picture-perfect dream.

In the same year as his failed tryout with the Packers, using his kicking abilities, Tom played on the practice squad for the San Diego Chargers. He never made it to the main squad that season, but he was beginning to make himself known in the league, despite his custom shoe.

The next season, Dempsey made it onto the New Orleans Saints. With his square-shaped shoe, Tom was able to show the world just how good he was despite the circumstances of his birth. In 14 regular season games that year, Dempsey made 33 out of 35 extra points. He only made 22 out of 41 field goal attempts that year, but most of his misses came from beyond 50 yards. He even went seven for 11 on kicks between 40 and 49 yards, but his longest of the season was from 55 yards. For his efforts, Dempsey was elected to his only Pro Bowl.

Despite his first full year being the only one in which he was elected to the Pro Bowl, Dempsey was not done leaving his mark on the league. On November 8, 1970, the Saints were hosting the Detroit Lions. Now, this was not the Lions of recent memory, but a Lions team that would eventually go on to make the playoffs with a 10-4 record.

Facing a tough opponent, the Saints struggled to generate offense for most of the game. With time ticking down, the Saints trailed by one point, but they were still well on their own side of the 50-yard line. Despite the NFL record-long kick being 56 yards at this time, they brought out Dempsey and the field goal unit to attempt a game-winner from a whopping 63 yards away.

Imagine what that looked like at the time. The ball was going to be held at the Saints' 37-yard line because the field goal posts were at the goal lines during this period of NFL history. It must have seemed absurd, even hopeless for the Saints and their fans in the stadium. But Dempsey took the field in his custom square boot.

With the game on the line, the crowd knew that it was a long shot, but they also hoped that their player could pull off the impossible, no matter the shape of his boot. As the ball was snapped, the holder was able to get the ball settled and aligned cleanly as Dempsey took his two quick steps toward the ball, using that straight-forward kicking method that most kickers had moved away from, and sent the ball into the air.

Players from both teams, the fans, and the referees watched as the ball tumbled end over end through the air until it came down between the uprights and only a foot or two past the center bar. As the ball came through, the back judge referee threw his arms into the air with such excitement to signal that the field goal had been a success that his feet came off the ground from the momentum.

Everyone in the stadium, even that referee, was jubilant after having witnessed football history. Tom Dempsey had shattered the NFL record for the longest field goal, and his attempt was even a game-winner. His teammates rushed the field and mobbed him in congratulations as the fans in the crowd roared their approval. It was a moment that marked Dempsey as one of the greats, especially considering what he had gone through to reach that moment.

Although that was the big moment that most remember, Tom Dempsey would go on to play in the NFL for nine more seasons. He would play for the Eagles, Rams, Oilers, and Bills before ending his career in 1979. Eleven years may not seem like a long career today, but it was well worthy of acclaim back then. And Dempsey's stats, although not spectacular, were still quite impressive when considering his birth defect. In his 1973 campaign with Philadelphia, he was a perfect 34-for-34 on extra points. His best season in terms of field goal percentage came in 1971 when he made just over 70 percent of his attempts.

Unfortunately, Tom Dempsey never made a field goal in the playoffs, going 0-for-4 in four playoff games for the Rams in 1975 and 1976. Still, his impact on the game was immense, and many still look to him for inspiration.

Some even accused him of cheating or having an unfair advantage because of his custom boot (which had cost $200 in those years, so imagine how much it would cost in today's dollars). Some thought that he was hiding a weight in that boot to help him kick the ball harder, while others said that the custom boot made kicking the ball easier because it provided a larger target to connect.

While many of these arguments have never been taken seriously by the historians of the game, the NFL did create two new rules because of Dempsey's impact on the sport. First, the field goal posts were moved from the goal lines to the back of each end zone, effectively adding 10 yards to every field goal attempt. They also specified that a kicker's shoe must adhere to specific measurements to prevent an artificial limb from giving anyone an unfair advantage.

Despite this second rule, a television show from ESPN set out to determine if Dempsey's shoe had given him an advantage. Long story short, they found that his shoe would have actually made it *more* difficult to be accurate and that it didn't provide any extra kicking power.

That's right. Tom Dempsey did all of that in the NFL at a disadvantage. Now, it is important to illustrate that Tom Dempsey did not have a Hall-of-Fame career. For many of these years, he struggled with his accuracy and overall fitness. His official weight was 255 pounds for a man standing just over six feet tall. There were even stories about him feuding with some of his coaches. Statistically, many of his season performances landed him in the bottom half of the league's rankings among kickers.

However, none of these facts can take away what he accomplished. Was his career a perfect Cinderella story?

Absolutely not, and no one should ever argue that it was. But what Tom Dempsey was able to do on a boot that was not standard to the NFL, with a foot that never had any toes to help with his balance, is still extraordinary.

That is why Tom Dempsey remains an inspirational story to this day. He was born without any toes on his foot, and he still became an NFL kicker. If you've ever stubbed your toe and haven't been able to put any weight on it, then you understand just how important the toes are to a human's ability to walk, run, or even remain balanced while standing.

Now imagine having to live an entire life without those toes. It's probable that 999 out of 1,000 people born without toes on one foot would just decide that playing a sport that involves kicking is out of the question. That one person out of 1,000 that decides to play a sport where kicking is required would likely never play it again after high school.

Tom Dempsey broke the odds on his condition. He demonstrated to the world that a birth defect does not have to be an impassable roadblock. If you want something badly enough, you can make it happen. Remember that Tom Dempsey's father told him: "Boy, you never say can't.

You may have to do something differently, but you can do it."

It might take you down a different path, one that no one else has to travel. It might seem unfair, or even hopeless. You might think that it isn't worth the extra trouble and that you should return to the path that the world has determined would be best for you and your situation. You could do that.

However, if you determine that you really want to reach that goal, then you can press forward, just like Tom Dempsey did. You can blaze your own trail and reach for greatness, even when the odds have been against you for your entire life. Just remember Tom's special boot and the special things he was able to accomplish.

# CHAPTER 2:

# 1972 MIAMI DOLPHINS

Many football fans have undoubtedly heard about what many call the greatest team of all time. The 1972 Miami Dolphins are best known for executing a perfect season, including a Super Bowl victory. However, few people are around today who can remember just how improbable the team's season had been. With that in mind, let's rewind the clock to the summer of 1972, as the Miami Dolphins prepared to begin a season that no one could have predicted.

It was only Miami's seventh NFL campaign, as the team had been founded in 1966. The first four years of the team's existence only produced 15 total wins, so there was not much momentum in their favor as the new decade began. However, when Coach Don Shula was brought over from Baltimore, things began to turn around.

In the 1970 season, the Dolphins finished second in their division and lost in the first round of the playoffs. Still, a winning season was new to this organization. In 1971, they advanced all the way to the Super Bowl, where they lost to the Dallas Cowboys by a score of 24-3.

Often, when a team is defeated so soundly in the championship game, they struggle to maintain their confidence and poise in the following season. Of course, this did not happen to the Dolphins. Despite the embarrassing loss to end their 1971 campaign, they came to the new season with confidence and determination.

The Dolphins opened the regular season with double-digit victories over Kansas City Chiefs and Houston Oilers, but they faced a stiff test when they traveled to Minnesota in Week 3. In a close match-up, they were able to score their only touchdown of the game in the fourth quarter, when quarterback Bob Griese connected with Jim Mandich in the red zone. The touchdown put the Dolphins ahead for the first time in the game, and they would hold on to win, 16-14.

Weeks 4 and 5 featured a couple of home games for the Dolphins, where they defeated the Jets and the Chargers by double digits. However, in the game against the Chargers, Miami's MVP quarterback, Bob Griese, suffered a broken leg and dislocated ankle after taking a hard tackle. Earl Morrall, picked up from waivers from Baltimore, was able to guide the team to victory nonetheless. Still, it was a big injury, and injuries are one of those uncontrollable elements in sports that make perfection so difficult to attain. Griese would be out for the rest of the regular season, maybe even longer. How would the team find a way forward?

Their third straight home game in Week 6, though, was another close game. This time, the Buffalo Bills came to town looking to dethrone the still-undefeated Dolphins.

After Ken Lee scored on an interception return for the Buffalo Bills in the second quarter, the Dolphins found themselves trailing 13-7 at halftime. The second half, though, featured rushing touchdowns by Larry Csonka and Eugene 'Mercury' Morris, opening up a 24-16 lead. The Bills would score late in the fourth, but they elected to kick the extra point, leaving them one point down and unable to score again.

With six wins and zero losses, Miami had made a name for itself around the league. It's important to recognize what happens when a team separates itself from the pack as Miami was doing. Other teams around the league would see when they played Miami and circle around, looking forward to the challenge. Professional athletes have pride. They do not like to lose. It's a personality trait that must be present for an individual to make it to the highest ranks of their sport. So, when they know there is a game coming up against the best team, they are more than ready.

But Miami was more than ready, too. In Week 7, with Morrall as the quarterback, they crushed the Baltimore Colts 23-0. It was a sweet victory for Morrall, as that was the team that had released him a few weeks earlier. However, the team's scoring was coming from the running game. Larry Csonka had two scores while Mercury Morris added another.

Week 8 featured another double-digit victory, this time beating the Bills in Buffalo. It was a strong response after the one-point victory just two weeks earlier. Miami was just getting stronger as the season went on.

This was evident in their Week 9 game against the New England Patriots. In the first quarter, the Dolphins scored 17 unanswered points and continued cruising through the entire game, which ended in a 52-0 score. In the rivalry between these two teams, this score remains the most lopsided game in their history. Coach Don Shula also became the ninth coach in league history to win 100 regular season games. Even more impressive, he became the first coach to win 100 games in 10 seasons. Every other coach who had surpassed the mark needed more games to reach the milestone.

Week 10 featured the Dolphins' second game of the season against the Jets, and they would need another comeback to secure the victory. After falling behind 17-14 at halftime and 24-21 going into the fourth quarter, Mercury Morris scored another rushing touchdown to secure the game for the Dolphins, beating the Jets and Joe Namath for the second time that season. More importantly, the team's defense held the Jets scoreless in the fourth quarter.

That had been one of the questions going into the season, especially because of the team's performance in the previous season's Super Bowl. In fact, the Dallas Cowboys coach at the time, Tom Landry, nicknamed the Dolphins' defense - the "No-Name Defense" because of its lack of star players. As often happens when a player - or group of players, in this case - is insulted by another team, they take that insult and use it as motivation. The Dolphins' defensive players took this nickname and ran with it. They knew they weren't superstars or marquee players. However, they knew that they could make a difference on the field.

To this point in the season, they had already tallied two shutouts. But, would their defensive strength hold up in the playoffs against stronger and more talented teams?

Weeks 11, 12, and 13 featured double-digit wins over the Cardinals, Patriots, and Giants. And, to cap off the season, they shut out the Baltimore Colts again. Bob Griese, who was injured back in Week 5, played in the fourth quarter of the game against the Colts, but he was not given the starting job entering the playoffs.

A perfect run through the regular season at 14-0 was complete. The Miami Dolphins became the first team in the NFL post-merger era to go undefeated in the regular season. Other teams have accomplished this feat since then, but none of them has done what the Dolphins were about to do.

On Christmas Eve of 1972, the Dolphins faced the Cleveland Browns in the divisional round. The Dolphins scored 10 quick points in the first quarter and held the Browns scoreless in the first half. In the second half, though, the Browns clawed their way back into the game, taking the lead briefly in the fourth quarter, 14-13. But the Dolphins were able to score one more touchdown in the final minutes of the game to win 20-14. The No-Name Defense came up big in this game as well, notching five interceptions.

Another unique aspect of the Dolphins' season came during the AFC Championship Game against the Pittsburgh Steelers. In today's game, when a team has a really strong regular season record, it gives them the benefit of playing playoff games in their home stadium. However, in 1972, home teams were decided by a rotating schedule. This process ended in 1975, but this year, it meant that the Dolphins had to go to Pittsburgh on New Year's Eve to play the Steelers.

The two teams went into halftime tied at 7-7. The Steelers scored first in the third quarter with a field goal, but the Dolphins answered with a touchdown to enter the fourth quarter with a 14-10 lead. The Dolphins' special team would block a field goal attempt, and the offense would score another touchdown, increasing the lead to 21-10. The Steelers would score one more touchdown, but they could not catch the Dolphins, who won the game 21-17. The Super Bowl was waiting.

For the second year in a row, the Miami Dolphins had reached the Super Bowl, which was held in Los Angeles that season. This time, the Dolphins were up against the Washington Redskins. As the game began, it quickly became apparent that whichever team's defense performed better would win the game. The Dolphins scored in each of the first two quarters while the defense held the Redskins scoreless, leading to a 14-0 score at halftime.

While things were looking good at the time, the Redskins' defense would not be outdone. Neither team scored in the third quarter, but the fourth quarter would have one dramatic moment. During a Dolphins' drive into Washington territory, the kicking team attempted a field goal. When Garo Yepremian attempted the kick, the Redskins defenders blocked it. The ball bounced to the ground until Yepremian picked it up and tried to throw it. He fumbled the ball in his hands and it floated into the air, where it was caught by Redskins cornerback Mike Bass. Bass ran the ball the length of the field for the touchdown, cutting the lead in half.

However, the Dolphins were not going to be deterred by the error. The defense held strong, and the Miami Dolphins went on to win the Super Bowl. The perfect season was complete. No other team before them, nor any time since - has ever played a perfect season. The No-Name Defense had won a perfect championship. Bob Griese returned from a broken leg to lead his team to victory.

One criticism of the Dolphins is that their regular season was full of particularly weak opponents. Only one of those teams would have a winning record at the end of the season. Had the Dolphins lost in the playoffs, their season would likely not be remembered for much today. However, they found a way through those stronger teams.

They overcame injury, insults from their opponents, and several losing seasons at their inception to become the most perfect team in NFL history. Teams today have come close to this record but have never made it all the way to the top. Most recently, the 2007 Patriots went undefeated through the regular season and won their way to the Super Bowl. However, they were upset by the New York Giants in the biggest game of the year, losing their bid to become the only NFL team since the 16-week season began to go undefeated through the entire season.

Even with a favorable schedule, winning every game in a season might still be possible, but the odds are pretty heavily against it. It's been over 50 years since the 1972 Dolphins accomplished this feat, and it might be another 50 before it happens again. The Dolphins' undefeated, untied regular season was the third in NFL history and the first of the post-merger era. The previous two teams to do so, the 1934 and

1942 Chicago Bears, both lost the NFL Championship game. The Cleveland Browns also completed a perfect season in 1948, including a league championship, while part of the All-America Football Conference (AAFC), but this feat is recognized only by the Pro Football Hall of Fame since the NFL does not officially recognize any AAFC records.

# CHAPTER 3:
# THE FOOLISH CLUB

Have you ever made a plan with a group of friends that seemed so foolish that people around you questioned if you were all insane? Maybe you wanted to accomplish some big goal, but the odds of success were very low, likely impossible. If you've ever gone against the odds, despite the advice of those around you, then you might find this story about The Foolish Club inspirational.

So, what did this group of people do that was so foolish? Well, it all began when two Texas oil businessmen by the names of Lamar Hunt and Bud Adams, Jr. decided that they wanted to establish two new teams to join the NFL in the late 1950s. Now, starting a brand-new sports team to immediately join the highest ranks of that sport is an expensive endeavor. Imagine the costs that go into paying the players, coaches, front-office personnel, and everyone else needed to operate a team. Then, remember that these teams also need stadiums!

Regardless of the risk and money involved, these two men pushed forward with their plans to bring the Dallas Texans and Houston Oilers into the NFL. They prepared everything they could to convince the league to let them in, but they were denied.

The NFL had turned them away, uninterested in their desire to join the league. Perhaps they considered the expansion to be too risky, or that they liked how many teams the league had already. Regardless, the decision was final, and the two entrepreneurs were shut out.

These two men were left with a decision to make. They could take their money and invest it somewhere else. They could find an organization that was interested in their endeavors and make a new partnership. Or, they could settle for what they had and forget the idea of owning a professional football team. After all, if you can't get into the league, how else could it be done?

Well, these two men decided that if they couldn't get into the NFL, then they would invent their own league: the *American Football League.*

Now, if you know anything about football history, you'd know that this was not the first time that a football league had been formed to compete with the NFL. In fact, this was already the fourth iteration of the AFL. Every other time it had been attempted, the leagues folded after a year or two.

Even today, there are still attempts to compete with the NFL in the form of the XFL.

So, how would this attempt be different?

To start, those two men from the beginning of our story went in search of more business partners. Hunt and Adams found several men who were willing to join their cause, and this group of men decided to name themselves The Foolish Club. Now, it's an interesting concept to take part in an investment plan that you know is risky, so much so that you decide to name your investment group something like The Foolish Club.

Imagine that you're trying to accomplish that big goal of yours, but you know how unlikely you are to succeed, so you nickname your plan something like the "Failing Idea." It doesn't exactly strike confidence in anyone observing your operation, but it does send a message to the world that says, "I don't care if this plan is likely to fail. I'm still going to give it everything I have."

With that mindset, The Foolish Club set out to prove everyone wrong. Each of the members of this group was either rejected by the NFL to become owners in that league, or they had minor shares of NFL teams, so they had the experience necessary to deliver successful results.

And they began with an immediate stumbling block. One of The Foolish Club members, Max Winter, who had committed to bringing a team to Minneapolis, actually pulled his team out of the AFL after participating in the 1960 AFL draft. Instead, he was lured over to the NFL, where he became the founder of the Minnesota Vikings. It was likely that the NFL had enticed Mr. Winter to join their side to intentionally weaken the AFL, but The Foolish Club would not go quietly. Instead, they looked for another potential owner to fill the gap.

In the meantime, the new league knew that one of the best ways to attract fans to their product was to collect talent. But, would they be able to lure players away from the NFL? Financially, they would be able to offer money to these players, but would those players take the risk of playing in a league that was not as established as the NFL?

Turns out, The Foolish Club and their management teams were very good salesmen. The AFL and their teams were able to sign 75 percent of the NFL's first-round draft picks to contracts. Most notably, the Houston Oilers team signed Billy Cannon, who had recently won the Heisman Trophy in 1959 while playing for Louisiana State University.

Imagine being an NFL team and using your first-round draft pick on a player you've scouted and learned about. You're probably very excited to add this young, talented player to the roster. You might even hope that this new player will help your team win a championship.

Then, suddenly, that player signs up with a team from a different league. At that point, you would realize a couple of things. First, you'd understand that not every draft pick is going to work out for your organization, especially if they never make it to training camp. The other thing you would realize at that moment, as every team in the NFL did at that time, is that this new American Football League and The Foolish Club were legitimate contenders for audiences around the country.

Everyone realized that this league had the momentum to survive. The Foolish Club wasn't so foolish, after all.

Still, over the next few years, the AFL and their team owners struggled to find their footing. During their first year, they only averaged about 16,000 fans in attendance per game while the NFL was consistently pulling 40,000 or more fans in each game.

The team established in Oakland, California needed a substantial loan from another team to survive their particularly low attendance for that first season, and it seemed to be an omen of things to come. However, some were gaining confidence in the league. After all, every single team in the league survived to come back for a second year, and that does not happen very often.

After a couple of years of decent results and steady attendance, the league and The Foolish Club landed a huge deal. In January of 1964, the AFL made a deal with NBC for $36 million, giving the league money it could use to attract even more players, and simultaneously bring a wider audience to the product. It was the deal that gave the league staying power, solidifying the AFL's place as a strong alternative to the NFL.

With that power, the league added a team in Miami, and they would add one more team, the Cincinnati Bengals, in the years before the league finished its run.

As the league strengthened, the NFL and its owners began bargaining with the AFL to stop them from poaching players away from the league. As those negotiations continued, the leagues realized that they were spending too much money against each other and that the battle was damaging both products. With that in mind, the leagues began discussing the possibility of a merger.

Mergers had happened in the past. Usually, one or two teams from a smaller league would join the stronger league, and the rest of the less successful small teams would fold and no longer exist. If that happened in this case, then perhaps some of those owners would become part of The Foolish Club forever, even if some of the original members abandoned them for the NFL.

However, The Foolish Club and the management of the AFL were determined not to let any teams fall behind. As the teams negotiated in June of 1966, they determined that the leagues would complete their merger in 1970 and that the two champions from each league would play against each other at the end of the season to stir up publicity for the merger.

These championship games were the birth of the Super Bowl. Unfortunately, though, the AFL teams would struggle to make their mark on the first two of these championship games. Infamously, in 1968, NBC cut away from an AFL game to show a children's movie. It did not instill confidence in the upcoming plan to merge the two leagues. Could The Foolish Club really be on the verge of letting everything fall apart at the last moment?

Cue Super Bowl III. The AFL's New York Jets faced off against the Baltimore Colts. On paper, the Colts were favored to win by as many as 18 points. They had only lost one game all season, and they had a very strong defense. They even crushed the Cleveland Browns 34-0 to advance to the Super Bowl. Meanwhile, the Jets had the worst defense of any division winner that season, and they had barely made it past the Oakland Raiders to reach the championship game.

Still, the New York Jets, with Joe Namath as their quarterback, defeated the Baltimore Colts in a stunning upset, 16-7. If ever there was a moment that proved The Foolish Club to not be quite so foolish after all, it was this game.

To make sure the world knew that the previous Super Bowl had not been a fluke, the AFL's Kansas City Chiefs defeated the Minnesota Vikings 23-7 in Super Bowl IV, another stunning upset. The Chiefs held the Vikings to 67 rushing yards in the game, something very rare for a team of this era to accomplish. Remember that rushing the ball was much more popular in those days, so to see a team not reach 100 yards was quite remarkable. But the Chiefs pulled it off, and they helped the AFL make their case to the world.

Both of those Super Bowl championships proved to everyone watching that the AFL and NFL merger would be a success, and the resulting product would be better for it. Each and every AFL team in the league was included in the merger, another first in football history. The 10 teams of the AFL were moved to the American Football Conference along with the Browns, Steelers, and Baltimore Colts. The rest of the NFL teams made up the National Football Conference.

The rest, as they say, is history. What started as a plan by a group of entrepreneurs looking to join the NFL became a long journey of risky business decisions and competition with a much stronger opponent. The Foolish Club took on the NFL when they were turned away, and to most observers, it seemed like a mistake. After all, there had already been an American Football League three times before, and each attempt by other groups had ended in relative failure.

Still, the men pressed forward, and the result was an NFL that now had a Super Bowl. Think of how big the Super Bowl is today. If not for The Foolish Club and their desire to own professional football teams, we might not have the American tradition of the Super Bowl. Not only did these people succeed in making it to the NFL, they unknowingly helped create a staple of American culture.

Every year, people gather around their televisions to watch the two best football teams in the league battle against each other for the right to be crowned as the *champion*. Millions of Americans watch in excitement, and advertisers spend millions for a few seconds of their attention. It's a spectacle that was born in the late 1960s, all thanks to The Foolish Club. Is there anything more inspiring?

# CHAPTER 4:

# JIMMY GRAHAM

If you're looking for an inspirational story that demonstrates how one's path through life is never a straight line, then you don't need to look any further than Jimmy Graham, a college basketball player for the University of Miami.

When Jimmy was a young boy, he had a troubled home life. When he was 11, his mother put him in a group home, as she was no longer able to care for him. In that group home, unfortunately, Jimmy was assaulted on numerous occasions by older children who also lived there. If you've ever experienced something like this, being abandoned by your parents, living alone in a new, unfamiliar, and unsafe place, or being attacked by others who were physically stronger than you, then you know the kind of scars this can leave on your body and mind.

Many people in situations like this often do not find much success later in life. Many of these struggling people will turn to troublesome lifestyle choices as a way to cope with the pain and stress. Jimmy seemed destined for this path of destruction if something did not change soon.

Thankfully, when Jimmy made it to high school, he began to find a path that was safe and loving, bringing him back from the point of no return. After visiting with a youth counselor at a local church for quite a while, he began to get his life back on track. The youth counselor helped him improve his school grades, and that stability helped Jimmy find the time and strength to begin participating in extracurricular activities. He quickly found that he could excel on the basketball court.

After being adopted by his youth counselor and becoming a basketball star at schools in North Carolina, he attracted the attention of college basketball scouts. That attention turned into serious offers. Serious offers turned into one accepted offer, as Jimmy Graham was headed to the University of Miami.

Unfortunately, basketball was not going to be Jimmy's path forward. Over the four years, he spent with the team at the University, Jimmy averaged 16 minutes of playing time, where he scored an average of 4.2 points per game, with 4.2 rebounds, and almost one block per game.

Jimmy had finished his undergrad studies at the University of Miami, but when he decided to stay for a year of post-graduate studies, he decided to try out for the football team, instead.

Imagine playing four years of college basketball, then one day deciding that you're going to give football a shot. It must have been intimidating, almost overwhelming, to try and learn football plays and formations, all the while competing at the college level. Even with this challenge facing Jimmy, he used his athleticism, speed, and size to make the team.

Jimmy was playing the tight end position, an offensive player who is big enough to occasionally block at the line of scrimmage, but is also fast enough to run routes and catch the ball when it is passed their way. It's a tough position, but Jimmy was doing his best to excel. In his one season playing for the University of Miami, Jimmy caught 17 passes for 213 yards, and he scored five touchdowns.

That season, the University of Miami finished with a 9-4 record, and they were ranked #19 in the college football rankings at the end of the year. Because of Jimmy Graham's strong performance, there were whispers that he could make the jump to the NFL. This is an impressive feat. Remember that Graham only had one year of playing experience, while most other players would have multiple years under their belts at this point in their careers.

This lack of experience likely affected many scouts and their assessment of his skill. He had a good season, but would NFL teams come calling?

Interest was there, but there was no talk of a first-round pick. As such, Jimmy Graham elected to participate in the NFL Combine, an event where prospective players participate in specific strength and agility skills to show the NFL teams their athleticism.

Scouts were impressed with what Jimmy had to show at the Combine, which included a 4.56-second 40-yard dash. However, they were still worried about his lack of experience with the game. Only one year of college play did not seem like it would be enough to survive in the NFL.

Despite this reluctance, Jimmy was drafted in 2010 by the New Orleans Saints, who used the 95th overall pick on the raw, talented player. The team negotiated a four-year deal with him, and his NFL career officially began.

During his 2010 rookie year, Graham was behind Jeremy Shockey in the depth chart, so he only started five games. Despite this lack of playing time, Jimmy still managed to achieve a couple of important goals. For example, his first receiving touchdown came in Week 9 when the Saints were visiting the Carolina Panthers. It was the first time he had played a game in the state where he'd grown up, and scoring his first touchdown there was a fitting moment.

By the end of his rookie season, Graham had established himself as a capable tight end, leading all NFC rookie tight ends in almost every receiving statistic.

At this point, many would consider Graham to be a success in the NFL. While he did not win Rookie of the Year or post any gaudy numbers, he was reliable for the Saints. Would he be able to build on that early success, or would he experience a sophomore slump and fade from the NFL world?

Well, this is a story of inspiration, so you can probably guess that Jimmy Graham was not done with the world of football, not even close.

In his second year, Graham put together a fantastic season. In Week 3 against the Texans, he caught four passes for 100 yards and one touchdown, marking the first time he had eclipsed that yardage in his career. But he wasn't done there. In Week 4, he topped his personal best by recording 10 more catches for 132 yards. He continued his streak of

100+ yards for two more weeks, establishing himself as an offensive threat in the league.

By the end of the 2011 season, Jimmy Graham had gathered 99 catches, over 1,300 yards, and 11 touchdown catches. It was the first time a Saints tight end had more than 1,000 yards receiving in a season. Furthermore, he tied the team record for receptions by any player in any position. That's how dominant he was. He had as many catches as any wide receiver in any season for the team. For his efforts, he was awarded his first Pro Bowl appearance.

He even helped the team win their Wild Card game against the Detroit Lions, but they would lose to the 49ers in the next round. Still, it was an impressive season, especially for a player who had now only played football for three years.

His 2012 season featured a couple more personal bests. He tied the team record for most consecutive games with a score in six games. He also had a personal best of 146 yards in Week 10 against the Falcons, which earned him the NFC Offensive Player of the Week honor. It was still a strong season, but he did not match his 2011 numbers overall.

At this point, some players might continue to decline or fall to an injury. It happens in professional football all the time.

Jimmy Graham could just become a fun story to eventually fade from the minds of football historians. However, Jimmy would continue to push himself to even greater heights.

His 2013 season began on a strong note. In Week 2, he caught 10 passes for 179 yards, a new career best. Week 3 featured 134 more yards and two scores, earning him another Player of the Week honor. But he wasn't done. Next game, he caught four more passes for 100 yards and two scores, which earned him a Player of the Month award. It was the first time a Saints tight end had ever been selected for the award.

As Graham scored so often at this point in his career, his touchdown celebration became famous. In an ode to his basketball past, he would dunk the ball over the crossbar of the field goal post at the back of the end zone. He even damaged one goal post in the process. The NFL would eventually make a rule banning this celebration, but Graham still did it one more time. The NFL fined him for it.

At the end of the 2013 season, Jimmy Graham led the NFL with 16 touchdown passes caught. He didn't just lead the NFL tight ends in this category; he was the leader of the entire league. He was selected to another Pro Bowl, and he earned the honor of First Team All-Pro. On a list of the NFL Top 100 Players, as voted by the players themselves, Jimmy Graham was 10th.

It's important to remember that he was not playing football six years earlier. Six years from zero to the 10th best player in the world.

His 2014 season ended with 10 receiving touchdowns from over 80 catches, as well as another Pro Bowl selection, although he did not match his numbers from previous seasons. After being traded to the Seattle Seahawks in 2015, Graham suffered a torn tendon and missed some time that season. He still managed a couple of touchdown catches that year, but recovering from his injury was more important.

Injuries can be hard to recover from, but Jimmy Graham did it with style. In the 2016 season, Graham had 923 receiving yards and was selected to yet another Pro Bowl. While his numbers were not as strong in Seattle, his 2017 season ended with 10 touchdowns, a team record for the position.

From there, his numbers continued to decline during his two seasons with Green Bay Packers and two seasons with the Chicago Bears. However, no one can deny the numbers that Jimmy Graham produced over his football career. In total, Jimmy Graham played 184 regular season games, where he caught 713 passes for 8,506 yards. Of those 713 catches, 85 of them were for touchdowns. In the nine playoff games he played in, he caught 31 passes for 402 yards and five touchdowns.

In the last couple of seasons of his career, he established the Jimmy Graham Foundation, an organization that works with veterans to help underprivileged kids experience what it is like to fly airplanes. The Chicago Bears selected Jimmy as their nominee for the Walter Payton Man of the Year award in 2021. While he did not win the award overall, a nomination from his team was still quite an honor.

Jimmy Graham had quite an unusual path to an NFL career. Most NFL players don't spend four college years playing basketball for a Division I school, waiting to play football until their post-grad studies. Most NFL players weren't adopted by their counselor in high school, or sent to a boys' home when they were just 11 years old. Jimmy Graham was definitely not most NFL players, though.

If there is anything to learn from what Jimmy Graham went through and accomplished in his career, it's that the path to success is not a straight line. In fact, it might be a path that no one else has ever traveled before. Is taking that new path by yourself challenging? Sure, it is. Is it easier to follow in the footsteps of your role models? Of course, it is. But Jimmy Graham did not have that privilege. He went through life with the skills and experiences given to him.

To say that he made the most of those experiences and choices is an understatement. Jimmy Graham demonstrated to everyone that the path to success always requires dedication, hard work, and passion to be great. No matter what your circumstances may be, you can find a path to success if you keep those key fundamentals in mind. Now that you've seen what can be accomplished, what are you going to do to find your path forward?

# CHAPTER 5:
## JOHN MADDEN

If you are a younger football fan, you likely only know the name John Madden from the popular video game series that features it. Football fans who are a little more experienced might remember John Madden's voice as he called out the plays of football games while they were being broadcast on television. Going even further back, though, John Madden was a successful NFL coach.

This story is about the life of John Madden, an individual who spent most of his life around the game of football in one way or another. With that dedication to the game, John Madden broadened the popularity of the sport while he helped, taught, and entertained his audiences.

Let's take a look at the football-filled life of John Madden.

After being born in Minnesota, his family moved to California, where John played high school football. In his high school years, he was a star player. He moved on to the college ranks, where he played one season at the College of San Mateo before earning a football scholarship to play at the University of Oregon. Unfortunately, that scholarship never worked out, as John suffered a knee injury that required surgery, effectively ending his ability to play at the top level required by that school.

Instead of playing at the Division I school, John played at San Mateo for a year, then at Grays Harbor College for another year before playing two seasons with Cal Poly, another university in California. If it was not apparent that John loved the game of football, then you only need to look at the topic of his senior thesis, which focused on how one can use weights to increase the strength of a runner's stride during athletic training.

Though Madden could play on both sides of the ball, his skill on the offensive line became quite pronounced as his college seasons came to an end. NFL teams took notice, and John was drafted by the Philadelphia Eagles in 1958. It was everything that John deserved after the dedication he had shown to the game, even with the loss of his opportunity with Oregon.

However, he suffered a collarbone injury toward the end of his senior season, so he was unable to finish his college career on the field. Another injury derailed John, but he refused to let the injury affect his morale as he continued to work hard.

John Madden made it to the Eagles training camp during the next summer, looking to earn a spot on the roster in

1959 despite the injuries he had already suffered. But, as it sometimes happens, the injury bug was not done with John Madden. During the training camp, John injured his other knee, meaning that with both knees at less than 100 percent health, his professional playing career had come to its untimely end before he could play one professional snap. It was tragic to think about, especially considering how much John loved the game. It certainly didn't seem fair that this man, who loved the game so much, would have the chance to play at the highest level just taken away from him.

While John would never wear the uniform and pads again, his injury did provide him with a path forward in the world of football, though it wouldn't be the one he thought he'd take. As he was going through rehab exercises for his knee, he saw another Eagles player by the name of Norm Van Brocklin watching and studying game film.

So, during his rehab work, John would listen to Norm explain what he was seeing on the game film and thus began John's journey into studying the game from the sidelines. Imagine finding that path, and using it as a way to deal with the pain and disappointment of your career-ending injury. It must have been invigorating to better understand the game from a coach's perspective.

As John was learning the game, he realized that he could put his degree in teaching to good use on the football field. One year after the knee injury that took him away from the NFL, John landed a job as an assistant coach for Allan Hancock College. After two seasons, he was quickly promoted to the head coaching position at that same school. As the head coach, now with a little bit of experience, John began to excel. In his two seasons as the head coach, his team had 12 wins and six losses. In his second season, the team had eight wins and one loss, and the team was ranked ninth in the nation among colleges of similar size.

John used this success to move up the coaching ranks, as he served as a defensive assistant coach at San Diego State University, where the school, again, found success with his help on the bench. Then, John made the jump to the professional ranks - but not quite to the NFL. The Oakland Raiders of the American Football League (see Chapter 3) came calling for a linebackers coach in 1967, where he helped the team reach Super Bowl II. After two seasons as the linebackers coach, he was promoted to the team's head coaching position.

As the head coach of the Raiders, John Madden found success immediately and regularly. Over the next 10 years,

John Madden would accumulate 103 regular season wins in 142 games. Among NFL coaches who have been on the bench for more than 100 games, no one has a better-winning percentage than John Madden. The closest he came to having a losing season was his last year as the Raiders coach in 1978 when the team had a record of nine wins and seven losses.

What's even more impressive about Madden's record is the era in which he coached. Some of his contemporaries included Tom Landry and Don Shula, whom most consider some of the best coaches of all time. So, not only did Madden win a lot of games, he did it at a time when he had to coach against some of the best minds in the sport.

The biggest achievement came in 1976 when the Raiders only lost one game in the regular season before going on to win Super Bowl XI. It was a championship well deserved.

In 1979, the next season after he had finished coaching, he signed a contract with CBS to provide color commentary for NFL games on television. He was paired with many different broadcasters initially, but the network found its dream team as Madden worked with Pat Summerall in 1981. These two individuals would become near-legendary to football fans, as their voices came through the televisions and into families' homes for a total of eight Super Bowl games.

In 1994, CBS lost the broadcasting rights to the NFL, which went to Fox, ABC, and NBC. Between the three companies, there was fierce competition for Madden's talents and personality. He eventually signed a contract with Fox for an amount that paid him more annually than any NFL player made per season. And he didn't have to take any hits!

Really, though, think about his impact on the game. John Madden's value to American culture rose above the game itself. By living a life that focused on the game at every turn, John Madden brought the game to every corner of the country.

# CHAPTER 6:

## THE MANNING FAMILY

It is a rare thing when more than one member of a family makes it to the highest ranks of a professional sport. It's even rarer when three of them do it. It's even more special that they all play the same position, as well. Cue the Manning family, an American dynasty when it comes to playing the quarterback position at a professional level. The three to have made it to the NFL include Archie and two of his sons, Peyton and Eli.

Archie Manning's path to professional football was tough, especially considering everything that happened around him. Let's take a look at Archie's road to the world of football and how he paved the way for his sons to follow in his footsteps.

Archie showed an interest in several sports, and he participated in as many as he could. Unfortunately, his father, "Buddy," was always busy working and could not watch his son play very often. Thankfully, Archie's mother was available to support him. While Archie was attending Drew High School in Mississippi, he exceled in every sport he played. In fact, he was drafted four different times by Major League Baseball teams because of the skill he showed on the baseball diamond. The Atlanta Braves drafted him in 1967, then the White Sox drafted him twice, and the Royals took a shot by drafting him in 1971. But Archie turned all of these offers down.

He had been attending the University of Mississippi and wanted to study and play football there until tragedy struck back at home. When Archie returned home for a summer vacation in 1969, he discovered that his father had passed away from suicide. At that moment, Archie decided that he would drop out of school, come home, and help his mom and sister by getting a job.

However, Archie's mom continued to support him by convincing him to go back to school and continue playing football, which he did. Imagine, though, what it must have taken for him to make that decision.

In college, Archie threw for over 4,700 yards, though his touchdown/interception spread was not great. He had 31 touchdowns to 40 interceptions, but his performance was still good enough to have his number 18 retired by the University. He was also named the Most Valuable Player of the conference in 1969.

When it came to Archie's move to the professional ranks, he was drafted with the second overall pick in the 1971 draft by the New Orleans Saints. He played for that organization for 10 seasons, though he missed the 1976 season due to injury. Unfortunately, the Saints never had a winning season while Archie was the quarterback. That didn't mean that he didn't perform well, though. In his 1972 campaign, he led the league in pass attempts and completions, though he also threw a career-high 21 interceptions.

After his time with the Saints, the rest of his career did not go very well. He started five games for the Houston Oilers in 1982, but he did not win any of those games. He started three more games for them in the 1983 season but also lost those games. Finally, he started two more games for the Minnesota Vikings in 1984 but went winless again.

His record as a starting quarterback was 35 wins, 101 losses, and three ties. This is the worst record for a starting quarterback with at least 100 games played in NFL history. He also never had the experience of playing in a playoff game, which speaks to the lack of strength of the teams he played for.

After his NFL career came to an end, Archie spent time as an analyst for New Orleans Saints television and radio broadcasts. More importantly, he later began working with his sons to host the Manning Passing Academy every year, where they give young players more practice with the passing game.

While Archie was playing professional football, he and his wife had three sons. The oldest, Cooper, was diagnosed with spinal stenosis while he was in high school, which prevented him from playing football any longer. Peyton and Eli, the two younger sons, both had paths to the NFL.

Peyton Manning played high school football at Isidore Newman School in New Orleans, where he had a 34-win and five-loss record as the starting quarterback. He wore the number 18 in honor of his older brother, Cooper. As Peyton's high school days were coming to a close, it was rumored that approximately 60 universities were looking to sign him up for a football scholarship.

Ultimately, Peyton elected to accept a scholarship from the University of Tennessee, where he went on to become the school's all-time leading quarterback with over 11,000 yards and 89 touchdowns. He also broke the Southeastern Conference's record for career wins with 39.

Although he never won a National Championship in the college ranks, he still attracted the attention of many NFL teams. With the first overall pick in the 1998 NFL Draft,

Peyton Manning was selected by the Indianapolis Colts. In his rookie year, he had over 3,700 throwing yards and 26 touchdowns, which was a record for NFL rookies. He also broke the record for interceptions by a rookie.

But he was just getting started. Peyton would go on to play 12 more seasons with the Indianapolis Colts. During that span, he led the league in completions twice, pass attempts twice, passing percentage once, passing yards twice, touchdowns three times, and passer rating three times. In 2006, he led the Colts to a Super Bowl by defeating the Kansas City Chiefs in the Wild Card Round, the Baltimore Ravens in the Divisional Round, and the New England Patriots in the AFC Championship.

In that AFC Championship, Peyton and the Colts had to come from behind, as they were getting crushed by the Patriots in the first half. At one point in the second quarter, the score was 21-3. This comeback of 18 points was the most in any conference championship game.

In the Super Bowl, things started off rocky for the Colts as the Chicago Bears' Devin Hester returned the opening kick 92 yards for the touchdown. Peyton did not help things by throwing an interception on his first drive. However, he made up for it before the end of the quarter with a 53-yard touchdown pass to Reggie Wayne. At the end of the first, it was 14-6 in favor of the Bears.

Manning didn't contribute any more touchdowns in the game, but their kicking and defense stepped up, leading the Colts to a 29-17 win over the Chicago Bears, bringing a championship to the Colts organization and earning Peyton a Super Bowl MVP.

After a Super Bowl and four MVP seasons during his time with the Colts, he missed the 2011 season to recover from surgery, then returned to the league with the Denver Broncos. He played three full seasons with his new team, including another MVP season in 2013 when he led the league in attempts and completions. He also set NFL records for yards and touchdowns in that season (5,477 yards and 55 touchdowns).

In his final NFL season, he struggled with injuries and only started nine regular season games. However, he returned for the playoffs and led the Broncos to a Super Bowl victory over the Carolina Panthers. It was a fitting way to bring his playing career to a close. His decorated career includes many individual records that he still holds, including the following:

- Only quarterback to win more than 12 games per season for seven or more seasons.
- Most games with four or more touchdown passes over a season, with nine.
- Most seasons in a row with 25 touchdown passes, with 13 seasons.

That is only a sample of Peyton's accolades, so be sure to look for him in the history books if you'd like to know more. There are plenty of examples to prove why Peyton is likely to be remembered as one of the best-ever players. For this chapter, though, there's still one more Manning with an NFL career to discuss: Eli.

Eli Manning attended the same prep school as his brother, but he put up much better numbers than Peyton had. He set school records in both passing yards (7,389) and touchdowns (89), then accepted a scholarship to play college football at the University of Mississippi, where his father played.

At the college level, Eli did not play much during his freshman year, as he was redshirted, meaning he could have one more year of eligibility. He took snaps in six games but didn't make much of an impact. The next season, though, he became the starting quarterback, and he had a successful season. He finished the year with almost 3,000 passing yards, 31 touchdowns, and only nine interceptions.

Although his team had a 6-6 record in his junior year, Eli still threw for 3,401 yards, 21 touchdowns, and 15 interceptions. In his senior year, Eli helped his team to their first 10-win season in decades. Along with all of those wins, Eli was honored with many accolades, including the Maxwell Award, which is given to the country's best all-around player every year.

When it came time for the 2004 NFL Draft, many expected the San Diego Chargers to select Eli Manning with the first overall pick. However, Eli and his dad, Archie, publicly stated that Eli would refuse to play for the Chargers because of their mistreatment of Ryan Leaf, a quarterback who had been drafted the same year as Peyton. When it came time, though, the Chargers selected Eli with that pick, then traded him to the New York Giants for Philip Rivers, a 2004 third-round pick, a 2005 first-round pick, and a 2005 fifth-round pick.

This began a 16-year career for Eli and the New York Giants, and while he sometimes struggled with consistency at times, he was a capable quarterback for the organization. In his first season, he only started seven games as the backup for Kurt Warner.

But, in the 2005 season, Eli took over as the starter. The team reached the postseason with an 11-5 regular season record, but they were eliminated in the first round. Eli threw three interceptions in that game, which did not help the situation. Overall, though, it was a successful season for the team. Questions remained about Eli's effectiveness, but the team continued with him at the helm.

After a mediocre 2006 season that included an 8-8 regular season and another loss in the Wild Card, Eli and the Giants went 10-6 during the 2007 regular season to reach the playoffs as a wild card. The Giants went to Tampa to face the Buccaneers in the Wild Card round, where they fell behind by a score in the first quarter before taking over the game, winning 24-14.

Then the Giants went to Texas to play against the Cowboys in a very close game. After being down 17-14 going into the fourth quarter, the Giants scored the only touchdown to win 21-14. The NFC Championship game was in Green Bay, where the Giants faced the Green Bay Packers. Manning and the Giants overcame Brett Favre and the Packers in overtime to advance to the Super Bowl.

Tom Brady and the New England Patriots were a formidable opponent, as they came into the Super Bowl undefeated for the entire season, trying to match the feat accomplished by the 1972 Miami Dolphins. However, one play in the fourth quarter stands out as the moment of the game. Trailing 14-10, the Giants had the ball and were trying to drive. On a third down throw, Manning targeted David Tyree, who was closely guarded but was able to pin the ball against the top of his helmet as he fell to the ground with the defender trying to strip the ball away.

The Giants would go on to score with 35 seconds left, taking the lead away from the undefeated Patriots and winning the Super Bowl. Eli was awarded the Super Bowl MVP for his performance, as well.

Eli continued to have success as the Giants' quarterback and even made another trip to the Super Bowl in 2011, where the Giants once again played spoiler to the New England Patriots. Eli was named the Super Bowl MVP once more, and his postseason performance set multiple passing records. His 106 completions, 163 attempts, and 1,219 yards are all playoff records.

After the 2011 victory, Eli and the Giants would only make it to the playoffs one more time in his career, which ended after a shortened campaign in 2019. In total, Eli Manning completed 4,895 passes for 57,023 yards, and 366 touchdowns. While he is remembered for not being as talented as his brother, his two Super Bowls ensured that he is remembered as an elite quarterback.

As this chapter comes to an end, it's important to note that there is one more Manning who may join the ranks soon. Arch Manning is the oldest son of Cooper, making him Archie's grandson. Arch is currently committed to playing for the University of Texas in 2023, but his career going forward is still in question. After all, making it to the college ranks is not a guarantee of NFL success. Then again, if he has been able to learn from others in his family, he might have the edge required to move forward.

Regardless, the Manning family has nearly made the NFL quarterback position into a family business. Some may argue that each of them had the advantage of having family there to help them move forward. This may be true to an extent, but no one is grandfathered into the professional ranks of a sport. Having support around you can be nice, but you still need to do the hard work. Each of the Manning players was willing to do that hard work, and that is an inspirational thought.

# CHAPTER 7:

# WARREN MOON

The path to the NFL for almost every player is very narrow. If you follow the sport, you know that players are often scouted as early as their eighth-grade year, all through high school, and then the college years, before they are drafted to a team to begin their NFL careers. NFL scouts have made a business of spotting talent as early as possible and then making sure those talented players are watched closely as they develop.

Every once in a while, though, a talented player slips through the cracks. This is often because some players unexpectedly make a large leap in their talent and development levels at a later stage than is typical. It's very rare for this to happen, but it's almost impossible for those unexpected players to make huge impacts in the league.

This is the story of Warren Moon.

Warren grew up in Los Angeles, California, where he lived with his mother after his father had died of liver disease when Warren was only seven years old. Because of his father's passing, and his mother being a working nurse, Warren would help around the house by cooking, ironing, sewing, and completing other housekeeping duties. While other kids would be excited to try multiple sports during the school year, Warren decided to only play one sport because he needed to spend time at home to help his family.

While it is impossible to know if these experiences impacted his future success, it is not too much of a stretch to say that when a person focuses their abilities and talents on one activity instead of trying a little bit of everything, then they might be more likely to develop more advanced understanding and skills.

It's also reasonable to assume that having to shoulder so much responsibility at a young age can often change the mentality of that young person. If it does not reach a tipping point, where stress causes the young person to spiral out of control, then the responsibility can help them with their decision-making skills. It seems that Warren Moon used his experiences to better himself, including on the football field.

When enrolling for high school, Moon was not zoned for a very good area. However, one of his mother's friends offered to let him use her address for his school application, allowing him to attend a better school. At Alexander Hamilton High School, Moon was named the starting quarterback as a junior. During his senior year, he helped his team reach the city playoffs, and Warren was honored with a nomination to the all-city squad.

After high school, Warren moved on to West Los Angeles College, a small two-year school, where he set several records as the team's quarterback during his freshman year. Despite his impressive performance, he did not generate a lot of interest from bigger schools. One school that did show interest, though, was the University of Washington. After transferring, Moon struggled in his first two seasons with the team. At the helm, Moon was only able to lead the team to an 11-11 record in those two years, but his senior season was another large step forward in his development and career.

The 1977 Washington Huskies finished their season with an 8-4 record, including six conference wins, which was good enough to claim the Pacific-8 championship. For bowl season, they faced the Michigan Wolverines in the Rose Bowl, where they emerged as upset champions. Moon scored two rushing touchdowns and one passing touchdown, earning him the MVP nomination for the game.

Throughout his college career, Warren Moon finished with a total of 254 completed passes for 3,465 yards and 20 touchdowns but also 19 interceptions. The numbers on paper were not great, overall.

At this point, with Warren preparing to graduate, most players bound for the NFL would be meeting with team scouts and hearing whispers about when certain teams might be looking to draft them. However, this is not what happened to Warren Moon. Many NFL teams were not convinced that he was of the caliber required to play in the best league in the world. As discussions continued, Warren discovered that if he were to be drafted at all, it wouldn't be until one of the very late rounds.

Warren Moon had a decision to make because getting drafted so late could prove to be detrimental to his chances to make an NFL roster. It wasn't often that a player who was fourth or fifth on the depth chart made it to the field.

Therefore, when presented with an alternate path forward, Warren Moon elected to take that unusual path. With the NFL draft approaching, Moon decided to sign a contract with the Canadian Football League's Edmonton Eskimos. This was a difficult decision because this alternate path was not a guaranteed way to make it to the NFL.

Thankfully, Moon was on a successful team. Moon split the position with another quarterback, and the Edmonton Eskimos went on to win the league championship five seasons in a row. During that streak, Moon was the championship MVP twice. He was also the first quarterback to pass for 5,000 yards in a single season, a milestone he completed just a few years before Dan Marino accomplished it in the NFL.

But Moon had one more accomplishment to achieve, which he did during his 1983 season. In that year, he threw for another 5,648 yards, which was another CFL record. In his time with the Eskimos. In his six years in the CFL, Moon amassed 1,369 completions on 2,382 attempts (57.4 completion percentage) for 21,228 yards and 144 touchdown passes.

While that final season was not successful for his team, as their record was only 8-8, Moon had successfully made a name for himself. With that in mind, he announced that he would be making the move to the NFL.

And for the NFL teams in need of a quarterback, the race was on. Who would be the winner in the competition to sign this talented star they all could have drafted years earlier?

After fierce negotiations, the winning team proved to be the Houston Oilers. In 1984, Moon's first season with the team, he broke the franchise record with 3,338 yards. The team struggled during his first year, but a new head coach Jerry Glanville was determined to find a way to better utilize Moon's talents.

The 1986 season was another struggling effort, but things began to shape up in 1987 when Moon and the Oilers finished with nine wins and earned a playoff spot.

Now, if you have ever played a sport at any level that has a playoff situation at the end of the season, then you know that these games have a different feel. There is a different sort of pressure that comes with playoff sports, and in professional football, the effect is even more pronounced. So, what would Warren Moon do with his first postseason opportunity?

He won his first game, as the Oilers beat the Seahawks 23-20, and Moon contributed with 237 passing yards and a touchdown. With a playoff victory under his belt, he went from being a good quarterback to an elite NFL quarterback, and he was likely ready to be paid by one.

So, before the 1989 season began, Warren Moon was signed to the largest contract in the league, and his skill for throwing the ball did not deteriorate. During his 1990 campaign, he threw the ball for more yards than any other player in the NFL with nearly 4,700 yards, as well as leading the league in completions, attempts, and touchdowns. He even threw for the second-most yards in any single game, with 527.

Also, during that year, Warren established the Crescent Moon Foundation, which worked to provide college scholarships to students who did not have the economic advantages that other students had. It was his way of giving back to the communities that were like his, full of individuals who just needed a helping hand to move forward. After all, if not for his mother's friend, he may have gotten caught up in bad decisions at a school that was more troubled near his home.

Moon would continue to have success in the league for a couple more years, one of them shortened by injury. In 1993, the team finished 12-4, but they were beaten in the first round of the playoffs by Joe Montana's Kansas City team. It was not a perfect, storybook season, but it was indicative of his successes while playing in Houston.

That season ended his time with the Houston Oilers, but he still remains the organization's leader in touchdowns and passing yards. Injuries would shorten his two years with the Minnesota Vikings, but he had a Pro Bowl season with the Seattle Seahawks in 1997.

As his career came to a close, Moon's final numbers were immense. When combining his NFL and CFL numbers, he finished with 5,357 completions, 70,553, yards and 435 touchdown passes. When he retired, he ranked in the top five passers of all time for yards, touchdowns, attempts, and completions. He threw the ball a lot, and he did it very successfully.

In all of his NFL years, Moon was selected to participate in nine Pro Bowls. While he never won a Super Bowl as a player, he was awarded a ring when he served as a broadcaster for the Seattle Seahawks, who won the Super Bowl in 2014.

He was also honored by the Tennessee Titans, which used to be the Houston Oilers when they retired his jersey number.

While Warren Moon was not a perfect individual, he did quite well in the NFL as a quarterback, especially considering the path he had to take. He was not handed a top draft spot, a big university scholarship, or even a decent high school. Warren Moon had to forge his own path forward with the help of his family. When thinking about the world of football, it's important to remember that the path to stardom isn't blazed by individuals. Those paths are most often created with love, kindness, and caring for one another.

Warren Moon found a way into the NFL, and when he finally arrived, he seized that moment and made the most of it.

# CHAPTER 8:

## VINCE PAPALE

While this may be a book about football players, this chapter is a bit different. This story is going to focus on a high school and college track athlete, a high school teacher and football coach, and a professional football player.

Instead of talking about a group of exceptional, inspiring people, though, this story focuses on only one person: Vince Papale, a man whose path forward was anything but traditional.

That's right. All of the individuals listed in the opening of this story are actually just one person. With this wild idea in mind, let's take a look at how this individual made his way through life to eventually land in the world of professional football.

Vince Papale grew up in Pennsylvania, and while he was a high school student at Interboro High School, he played football and basketball and ran track, all at the varsity level. He only played one season of football, which isn't much to build upon. However, he also only started running track events during his senior year, too, and he had some impressive results. In the pole vault event, his vault of 12 feet 9 inches was good enough to put him in the top 10 pole vaults of all time for Pennsylvania high school athletes. He also did well in the long jump and triple jump events, which set him up nicely as he transitioned to the world of college athletics.

Earning a track scholarship for his talents, Vince attended Saint Joseph's University in Philadelphia. In his sophomore year as a college athlete, he had some runner-up results in the pole vault and triple jump, but his junior year featured a pole vault victory at the US Track and Field Federation college development meet.

He also had some first-place finishes during his senior year, though he did not compete well at any of the larger, nationwide events. He was a decent college athlete at an average college, so there was nothing special about what took place. Vince was a good track athlete, but he would not be making the Olympic team.

Needless to say, Vince was prepared to move on with his life after graduating from the University with a Master's degree in Marketing and Management Science. He got a job working as a teacher right back at the high school he'd once attended, Interboro High School. While working as a teacher, he also took up the position of coach for the junior varsity football team.

While he was coaching the team and teaching, he saw that the Aston Green Knights, a team that played in the Seaboard Football League, was looking for players.

Before we go any further, it's important to highlight this part of the story. The Seaboard Football League was in existence for less than four years in total. It was formed in 1971, and it folded before it could finish its 1974 season because another league, the World Football League, formed and took away most of the talented players. That four-year window just happened to take place while Vince Papale was teaching at Interboro High School. Sometimes, the stars align.

It's also important to illustrate that Vince Papale had focused on track in college, meaning that he had not played a snap of competitive football for at least four years. It's difficult to imagine how he was able to overcome that gap in time to be competitive as a football player. He was competing against people who had likely played more recently and were probably younger than him.

But when the Seaboard Football League folded, Papale wanted to continue living out his dream. Instead of hanging up the cleats and calling it a career, he decided to try out for the Philadelphia Bell, a team newly formed that was competing in the World Football League.

However, Papale was 28 years old and had very little playing experience, as mentioned previously. When he tried out for a wide receiver position, he told the team's coaches that he was 24 years old. Vince was probably hoping that projecting youthfulness would make his value go up as a player because he might have more available years to play and grow stronger.

Now, this story is not suggesting that you lie and deceive others to get what you want. Instead, think of it this way: When you are working towards a goal, it is important to know what you need to be successful, and then find a way to meet those needs. Regardless, Vince Papale's lie would pay off for him.

He made the team, and during his first season, he caught nine passes for 121 yards. In fact, he was the first receiver in this new league to ever catch a pass. He also played special teams, where teammates were always impressed with his work ethic. In his 1975 season, he only caught a single pass, but that pass turned into a 49-yard touchdown for Papale.

With his strong special team performance for those two seasons, he earned some attention from the nearby NFL team: the Philadelphia Eagles. General Manager Jim Murray made sure that Vince was invited to a private workout with the team's coach, Dick Vermeil. During this workout, it's safe to say that Vince Papale impressed the coach - because Vince was signed to the team as a 30-year-old!

In the entire history of the NFL, Vince is the oldest non-kicker to play in the league without ever playing a snap at the college level.

As a wide receiver and special teams' player, Vince wore the green jersey of the Philadelphia Eagles for three seasons. He suited up for all but three games during that span, and he certainly wasn't kept off the scoresheet entirely. He was able to recover two fumbles, and he had one catch for 15 yards.

More importantly, he was respected by his teammates in the locker room. When it came time to elect a captain for each unit of the team, his teammates selected him to captain the special teams. He was also honored as the Eagles' Man of the Year in 1978, as the organization was very impressed by how much he participated in charities in his free time.

Unfortunately, his run in the NFL came to an end in 1979 when he suffered a dislocated shoulder against the Baltimore Colts in what was practically a preseason game. He would have missed eight weeks, and both he and his coaches understood that he would have struggled to make the roster after returning from an absence of that length.

Vince Papale's football journey was a difficult one and certainly not a traditional one. By all accounts, his early success with track and field would have indicated that path to be more reasonable and worth pursuing. But Vince loved, and still loves, the game of football.

In fact, he spent some time as the Treasurer for the Philadelphia Chapter of the NFL Alumni Association, a group that helps support former players and team members. His love for the game has not come to an end, and, likely, it never will.

So, what is there to learn from Vince's story? It's a tale that can be inspirational to those who have moved past the expected window for certain achievements or milestones. Just because you are a bit older than others who have progressed does not mean that you've reached the end of the road. There is always time to make a move toward your goal, and there's always an opportunity to take your shot.

Vince Papale demonstrated that the road less traveled can be a fruitful one if you're willing to work hard and make it happen. Not only did he demonstrate that to the world, but he also showed his son the same traits. Vinny Papale currently plays for the Memphis Showboats as of 2023, where he is listed as a wide receiver, just like his father.

If you needed any more proof that Vince's story is inspiring, the Disney Corporation made a movie about it, the Disney movie *Invincible*. Go and check it out if you'd like to see some of Vince's story told on the big screen.

# CHAPTER 9:

# NEW ORLEANS SAINTS VS. ATLANTA FALCONS, SEPTEMBER 25, 2006

The title of this chapter is focused on a regular season game, Week 3 of the 2006 season, to be precise. On the surface, it doesn't seem like there could be anything inspiring about an early-season match-up between two NFL teams, especially since more meaning is often attributed to games that take place later in the season.

To understand the inspirational aspect behind this game, one must fully understand what it means to represent a city. Many fans grow up learning to love the team that is nearest to their home. Fans and teams extend beyond the city, and the surrounding region becomes territory for that team. Think about your favorite teams. Chances are pretty good that your favorite team corresponds to the team nearest to where you grew up, although there are always exceptions.

Because of this love and dedication between a team and its city, those fans and citizens often look to their professional sports teams in times of trouble. Their team can often serve as a beacon of light when times seem their darkest.

New Orleans needed a light.

On August 29, 2005, Hurricane Katrina made landfall in the United States, slamming directly into the city of New

Orleans. In two days, 80 percent of the city was flooded, with some areas being buried in 15 feet of water. Many people were sheltered in the Louisiana Superdome, where the New Orleans Saints play, but the building had been heavily damaged by the storm. Over 1,400 people were killed, and many who lived were without their homes.

Even worse, news stories and rumors swirled about what was happening in the city after the storm had rolled through. Stories became politicized by some, and others wondered if the city was worth saving.

For months, the city struggled to recover. The Superdome was used as a shelter for quite a long time, so the New Orleans Saints were forced to play their home games elsewhere. Some argued that the people of that city had been abandoned by those who should have been there to help them recover.

It was a terrible, difficult year. This summary does not do justice to the history of the event, but it does explain why this regular season game was so important. It was the New Orleans Saints homecoming. Imagine being in the city at that time. Everyone was struggling and in pain. To make things worse, they could not go watch their favorite team play because that team was forced to play their home games in Texas. Even worse, you were likely hearing rumors that your favorite team might stay in that new area and never return.

Then, when the team finally did return, you were going to watch every second of their game. If you could get a ticket, you were going to attend the game. If you couldn't, you were going to watch it on television and make sure you saw every moment.

The New Orleans Saints had returned, ready to put on a show for their faithful fans.

Facing the same team that they had for their last game at the Superdome in more than a year, the New Orleans Saints were hosting Michael Vick and the Atlanta Falcons, a team that was also undefeated. Needless to say, the stadium was packed up to the roof. It was a sign of relief for the community, a sign that things were beginning to return to normal. It was a sign that life could move forward from tragedy.

But imagine the pressure on the home team. Think of how much it must have weighed on their minds. They wanted to play well for their city, a community of people who needed a beacon of light. They needed to win for the city of New Orleans.

Before the game began, there were performances from Green Day and U2, making the entire event into one large, raucous party. The fans were buzzing, excited for the game to come.

After kicking off to thunderous applause, the Saints began the game on defense, hoping to stop the electric Michael Vick and his scrambling offensive run game. On first down, the Falcons gained six yards on a handoff to Warrick Dunn. Not a good start, but the fans were still loud and cheering for their team.

Second down, Vick attempted a pass to Michael Jenkins, who slipped on his route, allowing the ball to fall harmlessly to the ground. It was then third down, and a chance for the Saints to get the ball back with a stop.

The ball was snapped back to Vick, who ran to his left in an attempt to gain time for a throw. However, the Saints' defensive front was quick to respond. They chased Vick almost to the sidelines before Scott Fujita knocked the ball from Vick's hand. As the ball tumbled toward the sideline, another Saints player, Byron Scott, had a chance to pick it up and run for the score, but the ball bounced through his legs and out of bounds.

It was a great play for the defense, although scoring a defensive touchdown would have been greater. Regardless, the punt teams were coming out for both sides, and the fans knew their offense would be getting a chance after the punt.

As the Falcons punt team snapped the ball and prepared to kick it away, a Saints special teams player by the name of Steve Gleason curled around another blocker at the line of scrimmage and found himself rushing straight up the middle of the field toward the Falcons punter. Gleason dove forward, both arms extended, and despite the Atlanta punter Michael Koenen's attempt to get the ball away in time, he kicked it directly into Gleason's block, sending the ball bouncing back toward the Falcons' end zone. Rushing toward the ball were seven New Orleans Saints players and Koenen. Falling on it in the end zone was Curtis DeLoatch, scoring a touchdown for the home team.

The stadium erupted.

This play would go down in New Orleans Saints' history as the revival of New Orleans. It represented a return to normal for a city that some feared would be lost forever.

The rest of the game went just as well for the Saints. After allowing a field goal from the Falcons in the first quarter, the Saints responded with a big pass from Drew Brees, followed up by an 11-yard rushing touchdown on a double reverse from Devery Henderson, a wide receiver who grew up and played college football in Louisiana.

At the end of the first quarter, the Saints led 14-3.

In the second quarter, after adding another field goal to their lead, the Saints found themselves on the verge of giving up points. With just under two minutes left in the quarter, the Falcons were ready to kick a short field goal to cut into the Saints' lead, but the special teams' game would prove crucial once again.

As the ball was snapped, one of the Saints' safeties was able to get a hand on the kick, blocking the attempt and preventing the Falcons from scoring once again. Thanks to a 51-yard field goal from John Carney as time expired at halftime, the Saints led 20-3.

The Saints added another field goal in the second half, but more importantly, they shut out the Falcons for the rest of the game. This included a fourth down stop in the fourth quarter.

The Saints had defeated a very good team - the Atlanta Falcons. They held Michael Vick, a superstar at the time, to zero touchdowns. The New Orleans Saints had performed for the fans in the stadium, and for every suffering person in the state of Louisiana.

As you likely know, the city of New Orleans still exists today. It was not wiped off the planet by a hurricane. The people and the culture of the city remain alive and well. The New Orleans Saints gave those people the best gift they could, which was a homecoming victory.

Much has been said about the devastation of Hurricane Katrina and how the United States responded to it. To this day, many have lost their faith in those who were supposed to watch over them, to help them stay safe, or at least respond quickly and effectively in the face of disaster.

They did not lose faith in the New Orleans Saints. And the New Orleans Saints demonstrated that the heart of a city could be revived from the brink of death.

Inspiration comes in many forms, but when a team can put a city's spirit on its back, it rises above the typical football story. Remember the Saints and their return to New Orleans when things look bleak. Never give up.

# CHAPTER 10:

## ROGER STAUBACH

Inspiration from the game of football is a beautiful thing. Players give it their all to inspire the fans and make those fans proud of the colors on their jerseys. However, few football players gave or sacrificed more than Roger Staubach did, as you will see, because very few of them would put their professional sports dream on pause to help their country in a time of war. Let's take a look and see why Roger Staubach is an inspirational story for anyone willing to put others first.

Roger was born in Cincinnati, Ohio, participated in boy scouts as a kid, and graduated from Purcell High School, a Catholic school. As he was preparing to enter a career in the United States Navy, Roger attended the New Mexico Military Institute for a year. While playing quarterback for that team, Roger scored 18 touchdowns and also set the school record for passing yards.

Now, most players who were experiencing success on the football field might look for ways to transfer to a school more suited to their abilities. A skillful player might utilize their talents to secure scholarships or garner the interest of better teams. Roger Staubach didn't do any of those things. Instead, Roger enrolled at the United States Naval Academy, preparing for his military career. He also played quarterback for the team, with his first snap coming in his sophomore year.

Unfortunately, his first performance was a disaster, as he was sacked twice and had zero-for-two passing on the day against the University of Minnesota.

Thankfully, the team's coach, Wayne Hardin, did not give up on Roger just yet. The very next week, as the Midshipmen faced Cornell, Roger was given another chance to prove himself. He did not waste that chance. Staubach passed for 99 yards and two touchdowns, and he ran for 88 yards and one more touchdown. The Midshipmen went on to win the game 41-0 in a rout. While Staubach was still competing for the starting role, he did get the nod for the rivalry game versus Army, and he rewarded his coaches for putting him in, scoring one rushing touchdown and scoring two more as Navy upset their rivals 34-14.

Things were looking up for Roger Staubach. Perhaps he would consider moving to another school to further his football career at this point. No, Roger stayed with the Navy and continued his military career while playing football.

In his junior year, Roger Staubach outdid his previous year's performance by a long shot.

The Navy Midshipmen opened their season at West Virginia, which ended in a 51-7 victory. They shut out William & Mary the next week before defeating the University of Michigan on the road, 26-13, in front of 55,000 fans. They stumbled in Week 4 against SMU, losing 32-28, but they rebounded against VMI in Week 6. One of their strongest opponents came to visit in Week 7, as the Navy faced #3 Pittsburgh. Staubach and the Midshipmen were up to the task, as they won 24-12.

At this point in the season, the Navy was ranked #4. But Roger was not done, as the Midshipmen would defeat Notre Dame, Maryland, Duke, and Army before the National Championship game against Texas. While Staubach and Navy lost, they still finished the season as the #2 team in the country. Roger was awarded the Heisman Trophy, which is given to the most outstanding college player every year. Basically, when a player wins this trophy, it guarantees a high draft position for the NFL. In his three seasons with the Navy, Staubach had 292 completions and 4,253 yards of offense.

Roger had his path to professional football on a platter, but he had different plans. He attempted to play his senior season but suffered an ankle injury that forced him to miss several weeks. After graduating, though, Staubach did one year on duty in South Vietnam in the Supply Corps before returning to the United States.

This detail of Staubach's life is particularly interesting and quite inspiring. While Staubach was studying and carrying out his military education with the Navy, it was discovered that he was color blind. This meant that he could only serve in the Supply Corps section of the Navy because it would not require him to know the difference between red and green. It also meant that he could have chosen to carry out his military duties on a base somewhere in the United States, where it would have been much safer and likely more comfortable. However, through all of these hardships, Staubach made the choice that benefited his country. He decided to honor his agreement with the military to the best of his abilities, even though he had many opportunities to go back on his word.

He personally elected to take the difficult, honorable path. Remember this when you're given the opportunity to take the easy road - just because you can, doesn't mean you should.

After finishing his military career, Staubach was ready to begin his tenure with the Dallas Cowboys, who selected him in the 10th round of the 1964 draft, even though he wouldn't be able to play until 1969. He was also drafted by the Kansas City Chiefs of the AFL.

He served as the backup quarterback to Craig Morton but took the starting role early in the 1971 season. After starting the season with a 4-3 record, Staubach led the team to 10 straight wins, the last of which was the team's first Super Bowl. Staubach was named the Super Bowl MVP after passing for 119 yards and two touchdowns.

After an amazing start to his career as the starter, he missed most of his 1972 campaign with a separated shoulder, but he returned in the playoffs to help the Cowboys secure a comeback victory over the 49ers. He would not be removed as the team's starting quarterback for the rest of his career.

The remaining years of Staubach's career included three more trips to the Super Bowl, where his Cowboys won once. The other two losses were both against the Pittsburgh

Steelers, and those two losses were by a combined eight points.

Unfortunately, the 1979 season would be Roger Staubach's last. It was estimated that he had suffered 20 concussions over his years playing football, and after having two of them in the 1979 season, he decided it would be best to retire before any serious complications took place.

Through his 11 years in the NFL, he passed for over 22,000 yards and 153 touchdowns. He also rushed for 21 touchdowns. He was also selected to six Pro Bowls during his time in the league. Many also credit him with the naming of the Hail Mary pass, which is a deep pass at the end of a game that only has a prayer's chance of helping a quarterback's team win.

Staubach threw such a pass during the 1975 playoffs when his Cowboys were trailing the Minnesota Vikings late in the game, 14-10. With time about to expire, Staubach fired a 50-yard pass into the air, which was caught by wide receiver Drew Pearson for the touchdown. When asked after the game about the play, Staubach reportedly said that he threw the ball into the air and said a Hail Mary, which is a popular prayer for certain Christian denominations. Ever since Staubach's story, the play has been known as a Hail Mary.

Besides the Hail Mary pass, he also earned a few nicknames during his career. He was often called Captain America because he was the quarterback for the Cowboys, a team often dubbed "America's Team." He was also sometimes called "Captain Comeback," because he tended to help his team find a way back into the lead when they were behind in the fourth quarter. Seventeen of his 23 game-winning drives took place in the final two minutes or in overtime.

Roger Staubach spent much of his life making decisions that others would not make. He did not take the road paved with gold that lay in front of him. Of course, making it to the NFL is not an easy accomplishment, but when he did have the chance to make it to the big league, he put it on hold to keep his commitment to the military. And when he could have served his military duties on a base near home, he chose to go overseas and serve as best he could.

Roger Staubach then went on to win two Super Bowls for the Cowboys, and we might wonder how many he could have won had he gone straight to the NFL after his Heisman season. But, there's really not much of a point in wondering, because Roger made the tough decisions, the honorable choices that very few others would be able to make. Those decisions are more valuable, more inspiring, than any number of Super Bowl rings.

# CHAPTER 11:

## KURT WARNER

When you're trying to make the NFL, but NFL teams tell you that they're not interested, that generally means it's the end of the road. Usually, it means that it is time for you to move on to other passions or other roads of opportunity. However, if your name is Kurt Warner, you don't listen to NFL teams, no matter how many times they say no.

Let's take a look at Kurt's path to the NFL and learn that just because the answer is no today, that doesn't mean that the answer is no forever.

Kurt grew up in Iowa, where he lived with his mother. At Regis High School, Kurt played football as the starting quarterback before moving on to the University of Northern Iowa. Kurt made the football team there, but he was very low on the depth chart for quarterbacks. In fact, he spent much of his college career as the third-string option for the team. In those first three years, he only threw 56 passes, connecting on 28 of them for 135 yards and two touchdowns. Most elite quarterbacks would get those numbers in a single game! It was as if his college team was already telling him that he was not going to amount to much, that there were better players than him, and some of them even attended this school. Kurt ignored them and continued to work, learning from those ahead of him on the depth chart.

As his senior year rolled around, though, Warner kept working hard and earned the starting quarterback spot. In his 12 games as the starter, he threw 296 passes, connecting with receivers on 173 of them, which was a completion percentage of 58.4. He had 2,747 passing yards and 17 touchdowns that year, leading the team to an 8-4 record on the season.

At the end of the season, Warner was named the conference's offensive player of the year. The question, though, is whether or not his one year of performing at a strong level would be enough to attract the attention of the NFL. The answer was mixed.

He was not drafted by any NFL team during the 1994 draft, though he did get an invitation from the Green Bay Packers to try out for the team during their training camp that year. Before the regular season began, though, he was released from his tryout by the team. It seemed that the answer from the NFL was no.

Needing to make money, Warner famously worked as a stocker at a grocery store in Cedar Falls, Iowa, making $5.50

per hour. He also began working as a graduate assistant coach with his former university football team as he continued to look for a way into the NFL.

For many of us, this would seem like rock bottom. We might think that we'd had our chance to try out with an NFL team, but we didn't do what needed to be done to make the roster. Instead, we were turned away, and it would probably be time to move on and look for a permanent job and begin living a normal, average life.

Kurt Warner was not ready to make that decision. During the next year, Kurt decided he would look for a different avenue in the football world, so he signed with the Iowa Barnstormers of the Arena Football League. Arena football is quite different from the traditional game, as it is played indoors in a smaller playing area. However, it still requires accurate passing, and Kurt was ready to deliver.

In his three seasons with the Iowa team, Kurt completed 62 percent of his passes for a total of 10,465 yards. He had 183 touchdowns to only 43 interceptions, for a quarterback rating of 107.84. He also led that Iowa team to two Arena Bowl games, though they were not able to complete those championship runs. It was a performance strong enough to cause a couple of important things to happen. First, he would eventually be inducted into the Arena Football Hall of Fame. Second, the NFL was taking notice.

It seemed that there was interest. Suddenly, the answer was no longer a negative one.

After his first Arena Bowl appearance, Warner asked for a tryout with the Chicago Bears, which they granted. However, he suffered a spider bite injury during his and his wife's honeymoon that prevented him from attending. Thankfully, he would get another chance after his 1997 season.

In December of 1997, Warner was signed to a futures contract with the St. Louis Rams, who sent him to play for the Amsterdam Admirals with NFL Europe. Unsurprisingly, in his 10 games with the Admirals, he threw for 2,101 yards, including 15 touchdowns and six interceptions, making him the top quarterback of that league. After returning to the United States, he was the third-string quarterback on the Rams for the 1998 season, only making an appearance in one game that year.

You might be thinking that Warner was never going to make it into the NFL. His draft year was 1994, and he was now going into the 1999 season. Five years of a potential career were gone. But Warner wasn't giving up, and the Rams organization saw his potential. He also spent his time while third in line studying the games of those ahead of him on the chart.

At this point in the league's history, there was an expansion draft, where new teams to the league were allowed to select players from other teams to help build their rosters. Each team were offered five players to select from the other teams.

The St. Louis Rams used one of their five selections to offer Kurt Warner. It was yet another sign that he was not valued by the team. From here, Warner would need a miracle to become a starter in the NFL. Then things started to happen. First, the expansion Cleveland Browns did not select Warner. Next, the second-string quarterback from last season left in free agency. This moved Warner up to the second-string spot behind Trent Green.

It is unfortunate when a player suffers an injury, in any circumstance. Trent Green tore his ACL during a preseason game, leaving the Rams with no other option but to name Kurt Warner the starter as the season began.

In Week 1, the Baltimore Ravens came to town, and Rams fans were nervous to see if their third-string quarterback from last year would be able to hold his own. They were not disappointed. Warner threw for three touchdowns and 309 yards to lead the Rams to victory. But he was just getting started.

The Rams would win their first six games, including a five-touchdown performance from Warner in Week 5 against the San Francisco 49ers, before losing at Tennessee and Detroit. After those losses, they won seven more in a row before dropping the regular season finale at Philadelphia. With a 13-3 record, the St. Louis Rams were headed to the postseason, and the world was finally recognizing Kurt Warner for the talent he demonstrated on the field.

That season, he threw for 4,353 yards, 41 touchdowns, and a completion percentage of 65.1, and he became the only quarterback in NFL history to throw three touchdown passes in each of his first three NFL games. For his efforts, he was named the NFL MVP at the end of the year. However, his team still had work to do in the playoffs.

First, the Rams faced the Minnesota Vikings in a high-scoring affair. Warner was nearly unstoppable, completing

27 of his 33 passes for 391 yards and five touchdowns as the Rams went on to win 49-37. Their next opponent, the Tampa Bay Buccaneers, had different ideas. In a low-scoring slugfest, Warner completed 26 passes for 258 yards, one touchdown, and three interceptions, but the Rams held on to win, 11-6.

It was the kind of gritty victory that might bode well for the Super Bowl, where the Rams faced the Tennessee Titans, a team that had beaten them during the regular season.

In a closely contended matchup, the difference came down to Kurt Warner's arm. With about two minutes left in a tie game, Warner threw a 73-yard touchdown pass to Isaac Bruce, and that would be enough to give the Rams the victory.

For the first time in NFL history, a quarterback had won the Super Bowl during his first year as a starter. It had simply never been done before. During that 1999 playoff campaign, Warner had thrown 77 completions at 63.6 percent, amassing 1,063 yards and eight touchdowns to four interceptions.

If it hadn't been official before, it certainly was after the Super Bowl. Kurt Warner was not only good enough to play in the NFL. He was an elite talent capable of rising to the level of competition required to win. He was an all-star player who just needed his chance to show the world.

At this point, some probably still wondered if this guy was the real deal or not. Maybe defenses around the league would learn how to stop his arm. Well, Kurt Warner wasn't about to rest on his laurels.

In an NFL career that would continue for 10 more years, most of which were shortened by various injuries, Warne continued to produce. In 2001, he was named the NFL MVP again, as he led the league in passing yards with 4,830. He also led with 36 touchdowns and a 68.7 passing completion rate.

Overall, at the end of his successful NFL career, Kurt Warner had thrown for 32,344 yards in the regular season, and another 3,952 in the playoffs. In 2008, he broke the NFL record for touchdowns in a playoff campaign with 11.

Warner became the only player to ever be elected to both the Arena Football Hall of Fame and the Pro Football Hall of Fame.

His accolades could fill several more pages, but the most important part of Kurt's story is how often he was defeated on his way to football glory. He is the only NFL MVP to stock a grocery store's shelf after his college football days had come to an end. He had so many reasons to turn away from the game that had turned away from him time and time again. He could have lived a normal life and just decided that an NFL career wasn't meant to be. But Kurt Warner made his own history.

He made the tough decisions and pushed forward. He used hard work to develop his skills. He used those skills to earn the attention of those who held the keys. He unlocked his own future. He worked with those who were ahead of him, learning from them, helping them learn, and overall being a good teammate while he continued to improve.

Kurt Warner is considered by many to be one of the best Cinderella stories in NFL history, and it's easy to see why. So, the next time you are told you aren't good enough, or that you don't have what it takes, remember that you have a choice to decide which way your story goes. You can choose to listen to the word 'no' and move on, or you can remember that just because it's a no today, does not mean that it will be a no tomorrow.

# CHAPTER 12:

## J.J. WATT

Often, an NFL player makes an impact on his team and positively contributes to the organization. He does the job he's contracted to do, and the hope is that he performs better than other players who play a similar position. This is the typical thought process when signing an NFL player. However, some NFL players seek to make a larger impact, not only for their team, but also for the fans, the community, and those who need help the most.

This chapter is going to examine the life, career, and impact of J.J. Watt.

J.J. was born in Wisconsin, and he grew up playing many sports, but his first passion as a kid was ice hockey. J.J. had played the sport from ages four to 13 until his family's schedule and financial situations could no longer make it work. With hockey no longer available to him, he began spending much more time playing football.

It's quite remarkable that J.J. was excelling at multiple sports in the fashion he was. It's not often that a young athlete finds success in two sports so vastly different in skill sets. Also, when you think about his future success in football, there is something special in the idea that he didn't fully commit to the game until he had already backed away from his first choice.

In high school, J.J. played football, basketball, and baseball, as well as track and field. At that time, J.J. played tight end on offense and defensive end on the other side of the ball. It was his offense that helped him garner some attention from a few colleges around the country.

After making visits to some of these schools to meet with the coaches and learn about the cultures offered by each school, J.J. selected Central Michigan University, mostly because of their head coach at the time, Butch Jones. J.J. was excited at the prospect of getting a lot of balls thrown his way, and Jones had convinced him it would happen at Central Michigan.

However, things did not work out between J.J. and this team, and after one year, he decided to transfer to another school. Transferring between schools was not as easy back when J.J. did it, so this was a big risk. Also, the school he transferred to, Wisconsin, had not offered him any sort of scholarship, or even a guarantee that he would make the team.

Thankfully, J.J. Watt was up to the challenge, and he walked onto the team as a defensive end. He was redshirted in 2008, meaning that he did not play so he could have another year to play later on, but he was able to play in 13 of the team's games during the 2009 season. And it was a successful season, as Watt had accumulated 32 tackles, 15.5 of those were for losses and 4.5 sacks. He continued to build on this success in his 2010 season, where he was the team leader in several defensive categories. In total, he had 42 tackles, half of which were for losses, seven sacks, and an interception. He also forced three fumbles.

After this great season, Watt decided to skip his senior year and declare himself eligible for the NFL draft, and again, he made the right decision. With the 11th overall pick, the Houston Texans selected J.J. Watt.

Unlike his entry into the college level, Watt did not have to wait before he began to make an impact. In his rookie season, Watt had 49 solo tackles and 5.5 sacks, 13 tackles for loss, and a couple of fumble recoveries. But, like his college seasons, he improved greatly going into his second year. In the 2012 season, Watt posted career-high numbers in tackles, and he led the league in sacks with 20.5. His 39 tackles for loss also led the league. Thanks to his fantastic efforts, he was named the NFL's Defensive Player of the Year, a title he would win two more times in his career.

Watt's best numbers came in his first five years before injuries would begin to affect his game. Some of the injuries he accumulated over the years playing football included a broken left hand, sports hernia, herniated disc, leg fracture, and a torn pectoral muscle. He always found a way to fight back and make his way onto the field, though. He even overcame an episode of atrial fibrillation, meaning that his heart was not beating properly. Unfortunately, although he finished that 2022 season, Watt ultimately decided that he would have to retire from the NFL.

As his career came to a close, J.J. Watt had collected quite the resume of statistics. His three Defensive Player of the Year awards were well deserved, as he had accumulated 449 solo tackles, 586 combined tackles, 137 assisted tackles, 114.5 sacks, and 195 tackles for loss. He also forced 27 fumbles and recovered 17 fumbles for his team. He scored one fumble recovery touchdown, as well as two interception return touchdowns.

Now that we've gone through all of his accomplishments on the field, it's time to examine the impact that J.J. Watt has made outside of the game. After all, NFL players are significant individuals in American culture. They have had an influence in the form of their fame, as well as the financial success that they experience from their contracts. As such, many NFL players have an opportunity to make significant positive changes, and J.J. Watt has done his best in that arena.

First, J.J. has created the Justin J. Watt Foundation, which generates funds to provide access to after-school opportunities for children, allowing them a safe and affordable way to play sports. To date, the organization has donated $6.8 million to schools all around the United States, giving kids a chance to achieve those sports dreams that they could not reach before.

For donors, J.J. and his organization have provided many Foundation events such as charity softball and golf outings, as well as tailgating events. The Foundation has been active since 2011, and each year they continue to raise money and donate it to these schools. J.J. has served as the president since its founding, demonstrating that he is not just using his name but is actively participating in the running of the program.

Outside of fundraising, J.J. has also been very kind and generous to those in need. In a 2012 game, after registering a sack, J.J. did a celebration that looked like he was sitting in a wheelchair and moving it along. This celebration was in honor of a family that had suffered a terrible accident, leaving two young boys handicapped, on top of losing their parents in the accident. J.J. had visited these children and grown close to them, and the celebration was J.J.'s way of dedicating the moment to them.

Again, when you think of an NFL player taking time out of his schedule, which is packed full of traveling, practicing, studying the game, and more, to give back to those who are hurting, it is truly inspiring.

He helped raise $37 million after Hurricane Harvey had devastated the city of Houston, where he had played for the Texans. He also reached out to family members after a school shooting at the Santa Fe High School, offering to pay for the funeral costs for those who had passed.

It's easy to see these athletes on television and assume that they live privileged lives, pampered by the money they make and the fans who adore them. However, some of these athletes choose to leverage their newfound power and create good in the world. J.J. Watt is one of those people.

Sure, one can be inspired by the defensive tenacity that J.J. demonstrated for several years in the NFL. You can find inspiration in his dedication to the sport, evidenced by the numerous injuries he had to overcome to return to the field. You might even find inspiration in the idea that J.J. Watt grew up playing travel ice hockey but ultimately landed on football.

There are plenty of aspects regarding J.J. Watt's life that are worthy of admiration, but his impact on individuals who need it most, without a benefit to himself, this is where true inspiration can be found.

# CONCLUSION

Individuals who make it to the NFL have already accomplished a great deal. After all, it is a rare thing to make it to the highest level of professional football, competing against all the people who want what they have achieved. But, among those who have made it to the best football league in the world, there are still ways in which a select few of them stand out. Some of these players look for ways to continue pushing forward because there is always something more to achieve.

This book has attempted to illustrate some of those great stories. Whether it was a kicker who was born without the toes on his kicking foot and had to make a custom shoe just to play the sport he loves, or a group of football owners wishing to challenge the status quo, thereby making the league a better product overall, amazing stories abound in the world of football.

Maybe you were inspired by the only undefeated team to ever show up on the field, or by a young man who needed help as he went through high school, only to switch sports in college and end up dominating the league.

Perhaps one of the most well-known names of the game was a story that warmed your heart, especially when you learned that he never played a snap of pro football himself. Or maybe it was a multi-generational family of quarterbacks that demonstrated how the love of the game can transfer down the family line.

Were you inspired by those who were turned away from the league initially, but continued to battle until they finally earned their spot, proving that they belonged there all along?

Finally, there is a good chance that you found something inspirational in the stories of those players and teams who took action to benefit those around them, whether it was a city in pain, kids who needed help, or a country at war.

The world of professional football is brimming with inspirational stories from its players, coaches, and even their owners. It's one of the things that makes professional sports so special; seeing how a group of very talented individuals can still find ways to differentiate from the rest, rising above those already at the top, to make an impact.

Made in the USA
Las Vegas, NV
18 November 2023

81058991R00069